THEN & NOW

FORT ATKINSON

THEN & NOW

FORT ATKINSON

Fort Atkinson Area Chamber of Commerce

This book is dedicated to all of the individuals—past and present—who have worked very hard to keep Fort Atkinson's history alive and to those who continuously work to ensure its future.

ISBN 978-0-7385-8274-0

Library of Congress Control Number: 2011930593

Published by Arcadia Publishing
Charleston, South Carolina

Printed in the United States of America

For all general information, please contact Arcadia Publishing:
Telephone 843-853-2070
Fax 843-853-0044
E-mail sales@arcadiapublishing.com
For customer service and orders:
Toll-Free 1-888-313-2665

Visit us on the Internet at www.arcadiapublishing.com

On the Front Cover: Noticeably unchanged from 1895 to the present day, Main Street represents the oldest street in Fort Atkinson, shown here facing south. After the first settlers arrived in the area, a wooden bridge was built across the Rock River, linking North and South Main Streets.

On the Back Cover: This image depicts an early-1900s celebration at the Chicago & Northwestern Railroad Company train depot along the tracks near the intersection of Janesville Avenue and South Third Street.

Contents

Acknowledgments

Project Lead is an annual program of the Fort Atkinson Area Chamber of Commerce, whose goal is to prepare individuals for public leadership roles through a series of monthly training sessions and the completion of a community project. It has been very rewarding for the members of our Project Lead XXIII Class to take on a task with such depth and longevity as this.

We used the Fort Atkinson Historical Society's efforts from past publications to shape us, guide us, and educate us in this endeavor. Their intent to keep the treasured past in focus is hopefully what we have continued to do with this publication, decades later.

We sincerely thank a number of supporters of our project. Museum volunteers—without whom, we would not have completed this book—include Kathy Connor, Wendy Haagensen, Nikki Knudsen, Ron Langellier, Kitty Welch, and Beverly Ankomeus. Also, we thank the Hoard Historical Museum and its director Kori Oberle for all of the time and in-kind donations they provided.

Generous sponsors of our Project Lead efforts include the Fort Atkinson Community Foundation, Fort Atkinson Women's Club, Fort Atkinson Rotary, Fort Atkinson Area Chamber of Commerce–Tourism Department, Fort Atkinson Wisconservation Club, Dean Brown, Jones Dairy Farm, Spacesaver, Joel and Linda Winn, Roger and Beverly Sherman, Lions Club of Fort Atkinson, Carla Haubenschild, James and Marie Beth Nelson, and Patricia Mitchell.

Much of the factual information in this book was derived from museum archives of the *Daily Jefferson County Union*, documented oral histories of area residents, books published by local authors and historians, and books published by the Fort Atkinson Historical Society.

The earlier photographs were all obtained from the Hoard Historical Museum's collection, unless otherwise indicated. The modern images in this book were photographed by members of the Project Lead Team in the spring of 2011. A historic review of the editorial material in this book was graciously provided by Sue Hartwick, the museum's former director for many years.

We also acknowledge all of the kind residents we spoke to and have gotten to know in this process, who helped bring the images and their history to life for us. Our mere curiosity about the past has grown into an unforgettable experience.

The 2010–2011 Project Lead Team members who created this publication are Julie Ankomeus, Carla Haubenschild, Jennifer Tucker, Kelly Jacobson, Nicole Miller, Lynn Sell, Eric Wipperfurth, Ryan Whisner, and Stacy Sherman.

Introduction

Comparing Fort Atkinson then versus now is a real testament to the founding members of our community regarding their vision, strength, accomplishments, commitment, and sense of community. Fort Atkinson still upholds these qualities, and as a result, we keep growing.

The *Koshkonong Country* volumes of the Fort Atkinson Historical Society (FAHS) state, "These volumes will indeed serve as a lasting contribution to the American scene and character . . . in order to make it possible for present and future generations to know of their past." We honor the FAHS by borrowing some of their words here, along with written pieces from the Fort Atkinson Area Chamber of Commerce and Hoard Historical Museum.

It is often noted that the period from 1830 to 1880 made America what it is today. At the outset of the 1830s, what has become Jefferson County was a total wilderness. By 1880, Jefferson County had become an important agricultural area. The population had grown from only Native Americans, trappers, and explorers, to 32,000 inhabitants countywide.

General Henry Atkinson built Fort Koshkonong (eventually named Fort Atkinson) during the Black Hawk War of 1832. Black Hawk was a Sauk warrior whose tribe inhabited the area at one time. The impressive roster of Black Hawk War participants included future presidents Zachary Taylor, Abraham Lincoln, and Jefferson Davis. It was the commanding general, however, whose name was forever attached to our town when in 1841 Congress declared us to be called Fort Atkinson.

During this time of carving out territories and establishing a sustainable living, many settlers came to the area or were invited by other family members who had heard about the lush living around the Rock River. Many of the street names we see today around Fort Atkinson were inspired by these early settlers.

The technological advances of this period were unmatched. By 1880, railroads ran through Jefferson County and the state of Wisconsin, connecting our area with all of the major railroads in the United States. Telegraphy, machine tools, farm machinery, petroleum, photography, the sewing machine, the rotary printing press, gaslights, and the cast-iron wood stove were all invented or introduced during these 50 years.

By 1900, Fort Atkinson's population was more than 3,000, and the new century saw a steady increase in business and manufacturing. Today, the population is more than 12,000, and the city is experiencing steady growth and prosperity and is a delightful place to live, work, and raise a family.

Much of Fort Atkinson's history is preserved in the Main Street and Merchants Avenue historic districts. Over 50 sites have been documented through the Fort Atkinson Historic Preservation Commission, Fort Atkinson Area Chamber of Commerce, and Fort Atkinson Historical Society as historic locations, buildings, and markers. Other registered historic places include the Fort Atkinson Water Tower, Hoard's Dairyman Farm, and Jones Dairy Farm.

Main Street follows the original military road between Fort Dearborn (Chicago) and Fort Winnebago (Portage), which was built in 1829. Our settlement was first surveyed by Milo Jones on May 18, 1847, using the intersection of South Main and Bark River Road (Milwaukee Avenue) as a starting point.

In the first decades of our history, downtown looked like a peaceful New England village, with small, mostly frame cottages and stores set among tall maples and elms. The Rock River split Main Street in two. There was no bridge in the earliest days, and the settlers went across the river on a ferry run by Dwight Foster, an early settler in 1836. He built the first frame house in the area, which still exists today near the Hoard Historical Museum.

By 1870, the first blocks of North and South Main Streets were largely commercial, but open spaces, trees between buildings, and an unofficial commons in the 200 block of South Main Street maintained a rural character. As the town grew in the late 19th century, the small frame shops gave way to moderate-sized, two- and three-story buildings. Constructed predominantly of the local cream brick, with Victorian arched windows, fancy cornices, and common party walls, they gave a new uniformity to the streetscape. The upper-story designs in decorative brickwork are attributed to the German masons working in the area.

At this time, the downtown commercial section stretched from Sherman Avenue to South Third Street. The edges of the downtown were marked on the north and south sides by the spires of the Catholic and Methodist Episcopal churches. Located nearby on the cross streets were service businesses, including livery stables, waterworks, tin and blacksmith shops, and a few industrial plants, as well as an opera house and city hall. The First National Bank, Citizens State Bank, and the Fort Atkinson Municipal Building are monumental landmarks, as well as the site of the Black Hawk Hotel and the Creamery Package Manufacturing Company.

As the community grew and word of mouth spread that Fort Atkinson was a sprawling place to do business, our city limits continued to expand and take shape. Beginning along the Rock River (current-day Milwaukee Avenue), many more businesses and residential homes were established, which led to the construction of a bridge to connect the northern and southern sides of Main Street.

Fort Atkinson is proud to be the home of William Dempster Hoard, the governor of Wisconsin from 1889 to 1891 and the man who is considered the "father of dairy farming" in Wisconsin. Hoard was a newspaperman and enthusiastic dairy promoter who started the *Daily Jefferson County Union* newspaper in 1870 and *Hoard's Dairyman* magazine in 1885—both of which are still being published today.

To help preserve our rich history, Frank and Luella Hoard gave their historic, c. 1866 home to the city in 1956, to be used as a museum. Now expanded far beyond its original size, the Hoard Historical Museum includes the Mysteries of the Mounds Gallery, the Lincoln Era Exhibit and Library, a local history collection, and many other exhibits. The museum complex, visited by thousands every year, also includes the National Dairy Shrine's Visitor Center, where guests can learn about the past, present, and future of the dairy industry.

Another historic feature near Fort Atkinson is the cluster of Native American mounds and effigy mounds located just south of town. Similar to the larger group of mounds at nearby Aztalan State Park, the mounds are an artifact of Mississippian culture in Wisconsin. Some of the mounds are effigy mounds, resembling birds and turtles. There is also the 125-foot-long Panther Intaglio west of town, the last remaining intaglio in the United States.

Today, Fort Atkinson is home to industry, healthcare, and a commitment to excellence in education, a growing tourist trade, and so much more. Our community definitely has a past, but it also has a prosperous, sustainable, progressive vision for the future. It is our goal with this book to entertain and enlighten you with just a taste of the rich history and remembrance that the Fort Atkinson Historical Society and others have kept, and to foster a feeling of kinship with the passion and dedication that is, was, and always will be—our community.

CHAPTER 1

All Around Town

In 1933, the local chapter of the Daughters of the American Revolution collected artifacts and stored them in the basement of the library. The collection grew, and the room was opened up to the public. So began the city's first museum. Today, the Hoard Historical Museum operates out of the Hoard home at 401 Whitewater Avenue.

The Panther Intaglio effigy mound was constructed by Native people around 1000 A.D. along the Rock River, west of the city. It was rediscovered in 1850 by Increase A. Lapham. The Daughters of the American Revolution and city officials led a campaign to preserve the landmark in 1920. The intaglio is the only one left in the United States. Shaped like a panther, it measures 125 feet long. It is intact; only part of the tail is hidden by a driveway.

The first white settlers arrived in the 1830s and settled on both sides of the Rock River. In 1842, a wooden bridge was built to link North and South Main Streets. The men of the settlement brought timber in from the woods and constructed the bridge themselves. In spring, during high water, the bridge was usually submerged. A concrete Main Street bridge was built in 1918. It has undergone many upgrades, but remains at its original location.

The US Post Office in Fort Atkinson has inhabited many buildings throughout its history. It began in 1838 in the home of Dwight Foster. Throughout the years, it resided in offices within other local businesses. On January 29, 1917, the new post office at 24 Milwaukee Avenue East was opened to the public. Constructed of mostly fireproof materials, this structure still exists today.

A bridge was built across the Bark River in 1852. Thereafter, hardly a year went by that the town or village did not have to appropriate some money to repair or replace the structure. In 1878, a new bridge was built at a cost of $362.98. The following year, it needed repair. These early bridges were made of wood planks and were soon worn through by the hoofs of animals and the weight of farm wagons.

The Chicago & Northwestern Railroad was finally completed in Fort Atkinson in 1859, thanks in part to Lucien B. Caswell's efforts. With a railroad, trade and economic growth could expand. Today, the railroad bridge is part of the Glacial River Trail. The trail is a scenic, recreational biking and hiking route that runs for six and a half miles, crossing the Rock River, gliding past the Glacial River Rotary Depot, and ending on Highway 26 at the Jefferson and Rock County line.

The Police Justice Building was located on South Main Street, next to what is Humphrey Floral & Gift today. In 1870, a village hall was erected on Milwaukee Avenue East, housing law enforcement and the fire department. Later, it was held in the Municipal Building, then on Edwards Street; in 2001, it moved to its current location at 101 South Water Street. The police force's dedication is demonstrated daily, and in remembering officer David McKee, who in 1968 drowned while attempting to rescue a teenage boy in the Rock River.

Fort Atkinson's fire department was organized in 1881. Before that, the city had fire wardens who arranged a bucket brigade and tried to eliminate fire hazards. By 1881, the growing city needed better protection. The city council instructed the newly appointed chief to enroll 120 men. In 1919, the fire department purchased its first motorized vehicle. In 1979, the fire department moved from its North Water Street location (behind the Fort Atkinson Municipal Building) to its current location at 124 Milwaukee Avenue West.

The City Hall Corporation was formed in 1882 to build what would become the Lyric Theater, or Lyric Opera House, on Milwaukee Avenue East. The building never actually housed city hall, instead serving as storage space for the city's fire department. The space was eventually used for Arcadia Lanes bowling alley, and the adjacent building became the Fort Theater. In April 2001, the need for public space gave way, and the structure was torn down, leaving only the front facade of the Fort Theater.

The first public library opened in 1892 on the upper floor of a building at 115 South Main Street. In 1910, it was moved into the former residence of Frank W. Hoard on the corner of Merchants and Milwaukee Avenues. In 1912, Henry E. Southwell, Dwight Foster's son-in-law, donated funds for a new building. In 1916, it opened, becoming the Dwight Foster Public Library. The library has undergone expansions since then, in 1931, 1983, and 2010, when the address changed to 209 Merchants Avenue.

The Soldier's Monument stands on a hill at Evergreen Cemetery, located on North Main Street. The monument was dedicated during the Memorial Day remembrance in 1898. In Lucien B. Caswell's address to the town, he stated that the statue was "intended to stand in remembrance of the soldiers who slumbered in the cemeteries of surrounding cities . . . and to all of the brave and heroic deeds that saved the Union from destruction."

Koshkonong Place resort was purchased by Arthur and Agnes Hoard in 1898 and was run by Hoard until his death in 1942. Called "the place to stay in its day," Hoard's Hotel was located on the eastern shore of Lake Koshkonong and hosted sportsmen who came to hunt in one of the premier duck hunting destinations in the United States. Hoard's Hotel became Koshkonong Mounds Country Club, which remains a popular area destination for golfing and dining.

The 1901 Fort Atkinson Water Tower was constructed to provide the growing community with pure water and adequate fire protection. It is made of 78.4 feet of locally-manufactured finished cream brick, the same style used in the construction of other local historic buildings. The elevated tank held 100,000 gallons of water and remained in service until 1988. Though no longer in use, the old water tower serves as a visual reminder of the beginning of city services and the birth of modernization.

The city fountain was originally installed at Jones Park around 1905. It was moved to Lorman-Bicentennial Park in the 1990s. It was removed from the park in 2003 and put into storage. In the fall of 2008, the fountain was restored and installed at Barrie Park in honor of local visionary Allan Haukom. Barrie Park is nestled between Barrie Street, Robert Street, Sherman Avenue, and Lincoln Street. Barrie Park's name comes from brothers Robert and William Barrie, who came to town in 1837.

The Black Hawk War Monument, donated by the local chapter of the Daughters of the American Revolution, is located at 407 Milwaukee Avenue East. The memorial was unveiled in 1906. The boulder still stands today, with an engraved plaque and wrought-iron fence around it. The memorial boulder marks the site of the original stockade fort, built by Gen. Henry Atkinson during the Black Hawk War of 1832, which became the site of Eli P. May's home.

In 1908, Joe F. Kaunzner worked just north of the present-day Fort Atkinson Municipal Building, at about 115 North Main Street, as a tombstone carver. He displayed his wares and chiseled orders right on Main Street. Today, the municipal building stands at 101 North Main Street, and Fort Tax Service is located at 117 North Main Street. Kaunzner's shop would probably have been in the space where the benches and clock stand on Main Street today.

In the late 19th century, the residents of Fort Atkinson debated whether they needed a second bridge over the Rock River. The most interesting argument was that it would help promote neighborly feelings and alleviate the "North-South rivalry" that sometimes flared up in town. The Robert Street Bridge was finally built in 1909. It was originally called the Wilcox Bridge and was often referred to as the "lower bridge." The bridge is still heavily used today.

Today, the Barrie Park Band Shell is hard to miss with its large, half-shell design towering above a small stage used for live band concert performances. The band shell's design lends itself to providing good outdoor acoustics during performances. The original bandstand (looking more like a gazebo in design) was dedicated at Barrie Park on August 17, 1927, to Joe Dietz, who had directed the Fort Atkinson community band since 1916.

McCoy Memorial Park is located off Highway 12, west of town. It was named in honor of Gen. Robert Bruce McCoy of Sparta, Wisconsin. A doughboy statue was dedicated to honor the soldiers of World War I and the Spanish-American War on May 19, 1929. The American Legion and Spanish War Veterans sponsored the project and appealed to residents for additional support. Originally a county-owned park, McCoy Park officially became part of Fort Atkinson in 2005.

A July 30, 1970, *Daily Jefferson County Union* newspaper article headline revered the "Municipal Swimming Pool" as the "Most Popular Spot in Town." The concept of a public swimming pool started in 1938, but did not come to fruition until 1955. Today, the Fort Atkinson Family Aquatic Center in Rock River Park includes basketball courts, paved parking, a waterslide, in-pool fountains, a picnic and play area, locker rooms, showers, swimming lessons, and programs through the Fort Atkinson Parks & Recreation Department.

CHAPTER 2

DOWN ON THE FARM

The Whitney farm is located just three miles up the east bank of the Rock River, in the Curtis Mill neighborhood. William Whitney, a Vermont native, came to Wisconsin in 1849 and devoted the early years of his life to farming. He later moved to Fort Atkinson, where he was instrumental in business growth.

On County Highway N east of Fort Atkinson, the Hake family farm was purchased on February 16, 1910, by Ben Hake for $4,000 at an auction. In 1938, it increased from 40 to 81 acres. The Hake family produced award-winning, purebred Holstein cows under the Cold Stream name. The family built a small cabin on their land, which holds a collection of artifacts, farming equipment, Native American tools, and family memorabilia. Ben's son Lloyd lives there today. (Then photograph, courtesy of Lloyd Hake and family.)

In 1902, George Hetts purchased land along the north side of Highway 12. In 1910, Hetts purchased two registered Holstein cows from Michigan, with the prefixes of Crescent Beauty, giving Crescent Beauty Farms (CBF) its name. The farm became internationally known for exhibiting and exporting cattle. In 1988, the cattle were sold, but the land was cropped for another 15 years. Later, the CBF Investment Company developed most of the land, where several businesses and homes are now. (Then photograph, courtesy of Hetts family.)

William D. Hoard was the 16th governor of the state of Wisconsin, from 1889 to 1891. He resided in a stately home, featuring Queen Anne–style architecture, on 604 South Main Street. Today, the home still carries its original style, but operates as Dunlap Memorial Home. Hoard passed away in 1918, and the home was lived in by his eldest son, Halbert. Halbert Hoard passed away in 1933. Dunlap Memorial Home was established in 1955.

Hoard's Dairyman Farm was purchased in 1899 by William D. Hoard. Hoard demonstrated on his farm that alfalfa could be raised as a successful forage crop for feeding dairy cattle. The farm continued to operate in a spirit of improving operations, and its success serves as a vital source of credibility for the *Hoard's Dairyman* magazine. The magazine's editors are actively involved in managing the farm today. The farm is located just north of the city limits on State Highway 89.

The W.D. Hoard Printing office still stands today at 28 Milwaukee Avenue West, named after its founder William Dempster Hoard. The *Daily Jefferson County Union* was founded in 1870, and *Hoard's Dairyman*, the only national dairy magazine in the United States, began in 1885. Today, *Hoard's Dairyman* magazine is published in three languages and goes out to 82,000 subscribers in 75 countries around the world. The *Daily Jefferson County Union* serves 7,450 in the Jefferson County area.

William Dempster Hoard's (1836–1918) advocacy of high standards for the dairy industry and promotion of farmer education were vital to the development of the dairy industry in Wisconsin. Hoard also launched the *Daily Jefferson County Union* newspaper, founded the national *Hoard's Dairyman* magazine, and served as governor from 1889 to 1891. Today, W.D. Hoard & Sons Company is owned by the Knox family, with Brian V. Knox serving as company president and newspaper publisher. (Now photograph of Brian Knox, courtesy of Ryan Ebert, art director for *Hoard's Dairyman*.)

In 1838, Milo and Sally Jones moved to Fort Atkinson from Vermont, carrying with them Sally's own recipe for pork sausage. Dairy farming is among the family's first business enterprises, thus the origin of the company name, Jones Dairy Farm. The 480-acre farm, located on Jones Avenue near Highway 26, is now dedicated to crop farming for corn, soybeans, alfalfa, and hay. (Then photograph, courtesy of Jones family.)

Original Jones sausage production began in the family's cheese kitchen. The house—with its original kitchen—still stands on the family estate and has been listed in the National Register of Historic Places. The farmhouse is still used for both family and customer gatherings and is located off a private drive near the plant on Janesville Avenue. (Then photograph, courtesy of Jones family.)

Jones sausage production moved from the house nearby to its first plant in the early 1900s. This plant was conveniently located along the railroad tracks. The second plant, at the current site on Janesville Avenue, was built in the 1960s. Jones Dairy Farm is now a state-of-the-art facility, still located on the original farm and still using the original sausage recipe. The original plant also houses the Jones Dairy Farm Retail Store, accepting visitors from all over the country. (Then photograph, courtesy of Jones family.)

Milo and Sally Jones's son Milo C. sold the first pork sausage in 1889. He started by sharing sausage, made with the family's recipe, with neighbors. His dedication to quality and hard work paid off as the business grew. Soon, he added bacon and ham to his product line, and orders are now shipped throughout the world. Philip H. Jones, the sixth generation president of the family-run, family-owned operation, maintains the same high quality standards established over 100 years ago. (Now photograph of Philip Jones, courtesy of Jones Dairy Farm.)

The Wilbur D. Becker farm, located on County Highway J, was established in the 1800s and remained with the family for several generations. The Becker family showed Guernsey dairy cattle as early as 1915 under the Fawndaway prefix. The family traveled throughout the southern states, loading their cattle into a railroad car to make the long trip. The family was also active in local Guernsey associations. (Then photograph, courtesy of Becker family.)

CHAPTER 3

WORKING FOR A LIVING

Northwestern Manufacturing Company began as Northwestern Furniture Company in 1866, producing furniture, but gradually turned its attention to making wagons, carriages, sleighs, and chairs. The factory space (all floors) totaled 65 acres. The company eventually went out of business in 1923. Today, on Sherman Avenue West where the manufacturing company once stood, is the municipal parking lot, boat launch, and 2 Rivers Bicycle & Outdoor.

In 1865, Oscar Cornish and David Curtis began a retail lumber business at the current site of McDonald's on North Main Street. They first manufactured the Curtis rectangle butter churns and wood silos. In 1884, Walter Greene became a co-partner. The proprietors' sons consolidated the business in 1898 under the name Creamery Package Manufacturing Company. Today, Five Star Antiques Mall and Rock River Canoe Company replace the building pictured on the southwest corner of Sherman Avenue and North Main Street.

Rennselaer Jay Coe came to town in 1869 and began planting strawberries on his 10 acres. By 1879, another 15 acres had been added, and Darwin Clarence Converse became a partner. By 1902, John Melendy Edwards's nursery business joined, and the company began as Coe, Converse, and Edwards Nursery, producing a variety of fruits and shrubs. The company disbanded in 1960, when Edwards's son Merle passed away. The main office, located at 43 Rockwell Avenue, is now Dunsmoor Doors.

Fort Canning Company was organized in 1901 and started canning a variety of vegetables. Because of local crop and machinery failures, it eventually specialized in corn and peas. In 1912, the factory output was 900,000 cans of peas and 200,000 cans of corn, which were shipped countrywide. Today, this area, located along the Glacial River Bike Trail, holds Jones Dairy Farm warehousing and the Fort Atkinson Food Pantry.

Lorman's Iron and Metal Company was founded by the Lorman family in 1914. The original shop, as pictured, was behind their home on South Main Street, facing Merchants Avenue. They collected and sold used parts and trapped furs. Scrap metals were collected by horse and wagon and brought to the plant. Loeb Metal Recycling purchased Lorman's Fort Atkinson facility in 1988, to purchase scrap metals from industries, peddlers, or individuals. Today, Loeb-Lorman Metals exists on Lorman Street west of Ralph Park.

In the 1930s, James Manufacturing Company (also known as Jamesway) occupied the space that is now the Fort Atkinson Police and Fire Departments, as well as their respective parking lots. Jamesway produced farm and barn equipment. Most notable was their production of cow stanchions, poultry incubators, barn stalls, and sanitary steel equipment. By the 1930s, they had another plant on Janesville Avenue near the current Nasco Arts & Crafts store.

Moe Light was moved to Oak Street in Fort Atkinson from Milwaukee by Henrik and Ole E. Moe in 1936. They manufactured lighting fixtures. During World War II, the firm was awarded many war contracts. In 1945, the Moe brothers retired, and Lee B. Thomas became president of the company. In 1953, the firm merged with Electric Sprayit and renamed the company Thomas Industries. In its place stands S.E. Smith & Associates and the former 5-Alarm Fire.

Nasco, first known as National Agricultural Supply Company, was founded in 1941 by Norman O. Eckley. His purpose was to list essential vocational-agricultural teaching aids in one comprehensive catalog. Today, Nasco International is located on the south side of Fort Atkinson along Highway 26 and offers products in 20 different catalogs. The original business was located along the Rock River on the northeast side of the bridge. Today, that space is a parking lot behind PremierBank.

CHAPTER 4

Home Sweet Home

John Quincy Emery was born in 1843. He built his home on the corner of South Fourth and South High Streets in the late 1800s. Emery was a prominent local businessman, involved in fur trading. Later, the house was moved to 331 Foster Street where it still stands today. The original site of his home is now the Fort Atkinson Middle School.

Eli and Eliza Ann (Curtis) May's home was located on 407 Milwaukee Avenue East. Eli May was a prominent resident, one of the founders of the First National Bank of Fort Atkinson, and a stockholder in the Northwestern Furniture Company. His home was built in 1863 on the approximate site of the original Fort Koshkonong. The home was constructed in Italianate style with decorative brackets and remains at its original location today.

Charles B. Rogers was a prominent attorney and politician in Fort Atkinson and an essential figure in the growth of organizations like the Fort Atkinson Historical Society, Fort Atkinson High School Alumni Association, and the Humane Society of Jefferson County. The Rogers home, as shown in 1907, is no longer standing. Today, the playground for the Heartland Preschool and 4K, on the southeast corner of Milwaukee Avenue East and Bluff Street, takes its place.

L. Marvin Roberts, founder of the Fort Atkinson Brickyard, inherited a farm from his father. He farmed until 1867, when he began manufacturing brick. In the 1880s, the Roberts family built their home at 505 Milwaukee Avenue East, using pressed brick. The wide eaves are supported with brackets, and the tall windows are accented with brick arches. The two-story bay window is common in this style.

Dwight Foster, the first settler in Fort Atkinson, arrived in 1836 with his wife and daughter. In 1839, he was appointed the town's first postmaster. Charles Rockwell originally built the home for $2,000 on Milwaukee Avenue East, across from the post office. The house was later sold to Dwight Foster, moved to the Hoard Historical Museum property on Foster Street, and in 1971, it was restored. It is Fort Atkinson's oldest frame house.

Robert J. Barrie was one of the earliest settlers and most respected residents of the area. He was born in New York in 1818 and moved to Wisconsin in 1837. He held various leadership positions in town. The early photograph is from the 1950s. His house was located on the 300 block of North Main Street and was often referred to as the Miss Marion Barrie house. The house no longer exists today, but Ten Pin Motors stands in its place.

Lucien B. Caswell came to Jefferson County in 1837. His 17-room mansion was built on the northeast corner of North Main and North Third Streets in 1873. The house was built by local mason Joseph Emery. The Caswell house became a landmark with its beauty and innovations. In 1919, the house was purchased by St. Joseph's Catholic Church, which later built a church on the same corner. Today, the site is a Walgreens drugstore.

The David and Jane Curtis house was built in 1885 and is located at 213 Sherman Avenue East. David was the son of one of the pioneer Fort Atkinson families and was one of the founders of the Creamery Package Manufacturing Company. Their house remains one of Fort Atkinson's finest examples of Queen Anne–style architecture and retains virtually all of its exterior features. It still stands at its original location today.

Monmouth H. Ganong was born in New York in 1830, and moved to Fort Atkinson in 1859. The Ganong home at 332 Merchants Avenue is a fine example of Italianate architecture. Ganong was a storeowner, ran a stagecoach line, and served as mayor. In 1866, Pres. Andrew Johnson commissioned him postmaster, and he served in that capacity through Presidents Grant, Hayes, Garfield, and Arthur. The house was remodeled in the 1930s, and a library was added in 1942.

Dry goods merchant George Marston built an Italianate-style house (with Queen Anne–style additions) in 1855 at 323 Merchants Avenue. Many people have owned the home over time, most notably Arthur Hoard, son of Gov. Walter D. Hoard. Arthur founded Hoard's Creameries and Bettersox Knitting Mills. He lived in the house from 1893 until 1942. The house was damaged by fire in 1980, but has been completely restored.

CHAPTER 5

THE ABCs

The Grove School was built in the late 1860s and located opposite Jones Park on Grove Street. It was later used as a city storehouse until 1947, when it was made into apartments for families of Fort Atkinson's military service personnel. The building was last described as a clubhouse for the city's senior citizens until its demolition in 1989.

The first schoolhouse was located on the southeast corner of South Third and Grant Streets. This structure was built in 1844 by Charles Rockwell for $100. In 1851, the school district was divided. Pupils from the south side attended school at this building while those on the north side held classes in private homes. Eventually, a school for north-side students was built in 1858. Rockwell Elementary, located on Monroe Street, was dedicated May 7, 1956, in honor of Charles Rockwell.

The first brick school building, the South Side School, was built for $2,000 in 1859. The first floor was used for elementary education, while Prof. John K. Purdy leased the upper portion for his private academy, or "high school," until 1866. That building served as an elementary school and gymnasium until 1903. Purdy Elementary, located on South Main Street, was dedicated May 7, 1956, in honor of John K. Purdy, who had also been the school district's first superintendent.

Caswell School, the first north-side grade school, was built in 1866 at the corner of North Third and Jefferson Streets. Constructed of brick for a cost of about $3,200, the school employed four teachers. The school was named after Lucien B. Caswell, one of Fort Atkinson's first lawyers. The second Caswell School was constructed at the same location in 1903. That school building was later converted into an apartment building and remains as such today.

Between 1898 and 1901, three new Fort Atkinson grade schools—Hoard, Barrie, and Caswell—were built. The Barrie Elementary School was first constructed on Robert Street. Later, it was used for the Fort Atkinson Vocational Technical School, which grew into Madison Area Technical College (MATC), which is now Madison College. In 1980, the school was torn down and is currently the parking lot for the Fort Atkinson Senior Center. The current Barrie Elementary School is located at 1000 Harriette Street.

James F. Luther Junior High School was completed in 1969 at 205 Park Street. Luther was the superintendent of Fort Atkinson Schools from 1950 to 1964. Students leaving the school in June 1998 were the last to use it as a junior high school. From 1998 to 2001, the building was used as administrative offices for the school district. It then reopened its doors as Luther Elementary School, becoming the fourth public elementary school in town.

The Emery Junior High School (located on South High Street) was built in 1927 on the site of the first Fort Atkinson High School, which burned down in 1888, and the second high school, which burned in 1926. In 1969, the former Emery Junior High was utilized as an elementary school, and then school administrative offices until it was torn down in 2000. The current Fort Atkinson Middle School is on South Fourth Street East.

South High Street in Fort Atkinson has been the site of public schools for almost 150 years. In 1866, Fort Atkinson's first public high school was built. That school was destroyed by fire on April 17, 1888. The second public high school opened in December 1888 on the same site. A third school was dedicated in 1912 and today is the Fort Atkinson Middle School. Fort Atkinson High School is now located at 925 Lexington Boulevard.

CHAPTER 6

SUNDAY BEST

In 1901, Friedens Evangelical Lutheran Church was organized by the Evangelical Synod of North America under the mother church of St. John's Evangelical Lutheran of Oakland. In 1902, the congregation purchased their first church. A new building was completed at 108 Milwaukee Avenue East in 1912 and still stands there today.

The First United Methodist Church was organized in 1839 at the cabin of Jesse Roberts. The first building was constructed in 1852. It expanded in 1865 and added a bell in the late 1860s. The building burned in 1890. A second building was constructed in 1891, but burned in 1928. Lost in the fire was the large Bible that had been in the congregation since its founding. The church was rebuilt at its 320 South Main Street location in 1929.

The Congregational Society, organized in 1841 at the residence of Milo Jones, held its services in homes and in one of the schools. The original church was built in 1852 on the southeast corner of Janesville and Milwaukee Avenues. The First Congregational United Church of Christ formed in 1854, and the original church was replaced in 1866 at its present location, 31 Milwaukee Avenue. That structure burned in 1942 and was later replaced by the present building.

St. Joseph's Catholic Church was established in 1884 as a mission of the Sacred Heart College of Watertown. The first local Catholic school was dedicated in 1913. For many years, Catholic churchgoers and students would need to visit separate locations for either worship or study. In 1956, the church and school were built together on the northeast corner of North Main and North Third Streets. Today, the church and school are located at 1660 Endl Boulevard. The building was dedicated in 2005.

THE OLD CHURCH

St. Paul's Evangelical Lutheran Church was founded in 1861, with the first worship center erected in 1863 at 301 High Street. The present tall Gothic structure was completed in 1901. The church started as an exclusively German-language-speaking congregation and transitioned entirely to English in 1956. In 1868, school was taught there four days a week. A 14-room structure was built at 309 Bluff Street in 1957, and a one-room school was built between the church and the parsonage in 1969.

The roots of the Episcopalian Church date back to Dwight Foster, one of the first settlers in the area. He was the first member of the church and died in 1870. In 1906, a mission was organized, with services held in the home of Edward C. Jones. The cornerstone for the building we see today was laid in July 1928. St. Peter's Episcopal Church became a parish in 1955 and is located at 302 Merchants Avenue.

Bethany Lutheran Church was organized as a mission church at 89 Monroe Street on August 16, 1942. In 1955, the parsonage at 728 Charles Street was acquired. On January 21, 1968, the new church at 404 Roosevelt Street was dedicated. At this time, the church had 55 children in Sunday school, 590 baptized members, and 395 communicant members. The building on Roosevelt Street is still in use today.

Trinity Lutheran Church had its beginnings in August 1942. The congregation began meeting in a room on North Main Street while planning for a new church. Construction began in 1949, by local contractor Will Pitzner. The building was constructed in a pure Colonial architectural style. On November 5, 1950, the building was dedicated. The church still stands at 314 Barrie Street.

CHAPTER 7

TAKING CARE OF BUSINESS

Business has always been a driving force in Fort Atkinson. Names of businesses have changed over the years, but keeping the business community strong has always been the goal of the community. The Fort Atkinson Area Chamber of Commerce has helped foster and promote business interests since 1899. Shown above are residents admiring the 1962 Creamery Package anniversary display in the chamber window.

These photographs compare North Main Street looking west between North Water Street and the river around 1920 and today. In the distance, South Main Street is visible. Today, the Rock River Canoe Company operates out of the same building that the Winterburn Drug Company did. The earlier photograph depicts the drugstore, First National Bank, the early US Post Office, a clothing store, shoe store, real estate office, fur trade post, and grocery store.

Dr. Frank Brewer used a home on the southeast corner of South Third and Foster Streets as a hospital from about 1903 to 1910. From 1921 to 1942, Dr. Peter James Majerus provided care out of a home on Madison Avenue. When Dr. Majerus ended his service, the Fort Atkinson Memorial Hospital Association was formed and continued hospital operation on Madison Avenue. The current hospital building, located on Sherman Avenue East, opened in September 1950 and has expanded since. (Then photograph, courtesy of Fort HealthCare.)

Today, the former Velvet Lips Lounge is situated next to the river on the corner of South Main and South Water Streets. This city block is made up of 88, 94, and 96 South Main Street. The three-story building at 88 South Main was built in 1886. The buildings at 94 and 96 South Main made up the W.D. Powell & Company meat market. The 88 South Main Street address was also home to John Westphal's Dry Goods Store and then J.C. Penney.

Some of the most important pillars in any community are its banks. The Citizens State Bank was chartered by the state of Wisconsin in 1884, located at 218 South Main Street on the west side of the street. The building was remodeled, including an Art Moderne facade, in 1937. Today, Citizens State Bank is now Badger Bank on Grant Street. Attorney Robert Bell maintains his real estate office in the old bank building, now referred to as the Bell Building.

On the northeast corner of South Main and South Water Streets sits a two-story brick building that has stood the test of time. Peter Imig constructed the building in 1885. Carl Becker offered dry goods including rugs, wallpaper, and men's clothes, until Harry Neipert took over in 1918. Neipert ran the store until 1976. Today, the same building still stands and is home to Jonas Office Products.

In 1921, Rex Knoepfel opened the first off-the-street gas station and operated it for more than 50 years at the northeast corner of South Main and South Third Streets. Before going into business for himself, he worked at James Manufacturing Company in Fort Atkinson. During World War II, when service station hours were limited by the government, he was employed at Creamery Package Manufacturing Company. Today, Brom's Tire and Auto Repair shop occupies its place.

In 1883, on the northeast corner of South Water and Grant Streets was Spaeth Brewery, operated by William Spaeth Jr. The brewery operated until 1919, when Prohibition forced it to close. Later, the brewery became the site of the Ebner Brewery, which operated until 1945, after which it became Clark's Tap. Then, Café Carpe opened at this location in 1985 and operates in the same building as the tap house.

Located on the northwest corner of North Main Street and Sherman Avenue West was Levy's Dry Goods Store. This photograph shows the Levy family standing in front of the store in the late 1870s or early 1880s. Later, this location was home to Creamery Package Manufacturing Company, then the Hartel Corporation; it is now owned by VyMac Corporation, which is the parent company of Verlo Mattress. VyMac Corporation restored the building in 2006 to keep its historic appearance.

In 1964, Dick and Betty Klopcic built a pyramid-shaped restaurant at 1131 Janesville Avenue and named it the Fireside after the fireplace at its center. By 1972, the Fireside had expanded four times to accommodate dining, private parties, and wedding receptions. A live, professional theater-in-the-round was added in 1978. The current configuration of the theater and gift shops was established in 1992. Ownership has since passed down to the Klopcic's son Rick and his wife, Jane.

The most prominent storefront in the older photograph is H. Hartman Hardware. Henry Hartman and Lyman Jeffords formed their partnership in 1924 and ran the hardware store with a specialty of heating and plumbing supplies. The hardware store was located on the east side of North Main Street. The store was torn down and replaced with First National Bank (now PremierBank). Other businesses in the old photograph include Felbel's General Store, Geisel's Tailor Shop, Ott's Grocery Store, and Statz's Grocery Store.

At 15 South Third Street East on what is now the parking lot behind the post office stood Fort Transportation & Service Company. The original company was founded by Fred Koester in the 1880s and continued by John Koester in March 1925. The transportation company hauled supplies from the railroad to merchants in town. The company moved to 1600 Janesville Avenue in 1971 and spawned R&H Services to service trucks. It became Fort Transportation in 1985, providing truckload services and warehousing.

William Lohmaier constructed the building occupied by William Reap's Saloon in 1896. Saloons and taverns were plentiful before Prohibition worked its way into the city. The 18th Amendment made Prohibition effective nationwide, and the bars in Fort Atkinson closed on July 1, 1919. Since then, the building housed many different shops, namely bakeshops. At one point, it was the Fort Bakery. Today, for more than 50 years, it has operated as the family-owned business Krueger Jewelers at 106 North Main Street.

At 234 South Main Street sat Bartelt Furniture Store, started in 1910. The store started with a small space, but expanded in 1928 to having one of the largest display spaces in town. Maintaining a tradition of furniture sales, High Point Properties ran the Ravenwood Fine Furniture store through 2010. Most recently, Furniture Outlet occupied this location.

It may be difficult to tell today, but part of the Humphrey Floral & Gift building on Main Street used to be a chicken hatchery. The Mueller-Cory Hatchery stood at 203 South Main Street in 1919. The business was hatching and selling day-old chicks. Using a 20,000-egg incubator, about 3,000 chicks could be turned in a day during the hatching season. It was reported in 1930 that 107 birds at the hatchery could produce 2,318 eggs.

In July 1953, the Great Atlantic & Pacific Tea Company, often referred to as the local A&P, opened its doors in downtown Fort Atkinson. The building was originally constructed in 1871, housed the Langhoff Farmer's Market & Saloon, and was often referred to as the Langhoff building. Today, the Bolt Inn tavern sits at 225 South Main Street and American Family Insurance at 229 South Main Street. Both locations represent where the A&P once stood.

Growing communities thrive when they make goods and services available for their residents. Fort Atkinson has welcomed many grocery stores over time. Early in the development of bustling Main Street, Smith's Store stood between the Black Hawk Hotel and the First Congregational United Church of Christ on Milwaukee Avenue West. A building still stands there today between what is now the Black Hawk Tavern & Grille, Black Hawk Senior Residence, and the church.

The original Blodgett's Mill was located at 10 Madison Avenue. It was owned by three generations of the Hoffman family, who also owned an adjacent lumberyard. In 1954, Ted Blodgett and his son Jack purchased the business as part of the mill and rented the building from the Hoffman family. Today, Goyer's Ace Hardware stands where Blodgett's Mill and Hoffman Lumber Company used to be. Blodgett Garden Center still operates today, out on Janesville Avenue.

The Project Lead Team appears "then" and "now." In both photographs, they are, from left to right, top to bottom, Dean Brown (president, Fort Atkinson Area Chamber of Commerce), Ryan Whisner, Jennifer Tucker, Julie Ankomeus, Stacy Sherman, Lynn Forseth (Project Lead facilitator and executive director of Workforce and Economic Development, Madison Area Technical College), Dianne Hrobsky (executive vice president, Fort Atkinson Area Chamber of Commerce), Carla Haubenschild, Nicole Miller, Lynn Sell, Kelly Jacobson, and Eric Wipperfurth.